A Life Above Water

A Life Above Water

Poems

Doug Van Gundy

RED HEN PRESS | *Los Angeles, California*

A Life Above Water

Book design by Mark E. Cull

ISBN: 978-1-59709-431-3
Library of Congress Catalog Card Number: 2007920077

The City of Los Angeles Department of Cultural Affairs, Los Angeles County Arts Commission and National Endowment for the Arts partially support Red Hen Press.

Published by Red Hen Press
First Edition

for Melissa

Acknowledgements

Some of these poems first appeared, often in slightly different versions, in the following magazines, to whose editors a grateful acknowledgment is made: *Coastal Forest Review, CrossConnect, Kestrel, Lullwater Review, Negative Capability.*

Additionally, the poems "The Still, Small Voice" and "A Beautiful Jar of Jelly" were included in the anthology, *Wild Sweet Notes: Fifty Years of West Virginia Poetry* (2000, Publisher's Place).

Special Thanks to: My parents, Jim and Judy Van Gundy; Jim Peterson, Peg Davis, Joan Larkin, Jim Clark, Ken Waldman, Nora Mitchell, John Goughneour, Kirk Judd, Dwight Diller, Kate Gale and Mark Cull at Red Hen Press; and especially my sweet wife, Melissa.

Contents

The Great Slowing

All These Indigestible Parts

*It isn't
innocence I find in them, but a fathoming
depth of attention anchored in the heart, in its
whorl of blood and muscle beating round.*

—Eamon Grennan
"A Closer Look"

Keeper

I am too small to concern him.
He is seeking sleeker, keeper-sized fish:
spotted brown trout and iridescent rainbows.

From beneath the water, I cannot see the line to which the fly is tied,
only his liquid arms, the slow smooth motion of back casting and roll casting,
the pause and the presentation.

I have been watching him for hours,
and have seen the larger fish pulled into the sky,
kissed and then released.
I have raced to their sides to ask them what it's like.

"*It's like dying*" one says. And then, "*It's beautiful.*
If only I could breathe up there. You can't
imagine the taste of air on your skin
and the sweet heavy sensation of feeling your own weight."
He drifts to a dark place beneath a sandstone ledge
to dream of a life above water.

I long to live in my father's sky,
in his world of clouds and boots and moss-lined creels.
In that moment I will be large enough to keep,
large enough that he will tuck me into his creel,
carry me home, and teach me the language
that lives inside new lungs.

Pipistrelle

His winged corpse is laid out
in the traditional manner, on a bed
of green spruce needles, a squirrel-
gnawed cone supporting his slight head.
His wings are outstretched, mouth agape.
The heatless January sun illuminates
his leathery tailflap.

The ceremony is simple,
his earth-bound body is bathed
by tender tongues, his soft bat-wool combed
by smooth teeth and wing spurs. Then the gathered
sing his slender carcass poem,
the whole of the song
weighing less than an ounce.

When the singing is finished and the mourners
have dispersed, his remains are left behind. The insects
that have lived long in fear
of his silent, screeching flight
are able to exact their revenge, to take sustenance from his insect-
fed flesh.

Knapp's Creek

It was still way back in the throat
of Sunday morning when I stole out of the house,
crossed the low ridge of Hamilton Hill,
and lowered myself onto the banks of the creek.
Deep in the bottom of the valley,
along the liquid place where falling down
becomes climbing up,
I lay on a smooth block of sandstone
and listened to that part of the world
that was not me.

Upstream, the satisfied sound
of stones being stroked by water,
the voice of their pleasure straining toward human language.
Downstream, the rocks in the water speak in algae,
the rocks on the shoreline speak in moss:
their affection, each for the other, dissolved
with the loss of a common tongue,

And here, in a backwater just below my feet,
surrounded by hundreds of sunken poplar leaves
like the drowned shadows of long-dead birds,
in this place where the rocks flow slower than the river,
a pregnant stone is poised to give birth
in the direction of the sea.

Chipmunk

So it turns out the sound I took to be some game
Hen, that distant and satisfying wood-block clucking
Was in fact the sound of a chipmunk calling
Out from beneath the rock upon which I was sitting.

Surprised at first by the dry leaf rustle
And then by the sight of him, his cheeks unpuffing
And puffing in correspondence with that hollow,
Blonde sound, I was looking straight down

Upon him, sitting breathlessly for fear
He would register any movement
In his cave-black prey eyes and, taking me
For a hawk or fox, vanish.

Of course, he did vanish, But not before
I was able to witness him
In all his utter chipmunkness—darting
From under the rock, sniffing the air, twitching

His tail like a seismograph needle; waiting. After
He disappeared, I watched for his reappearance
Intently. Beneath the boulder, I could hear his tiny
Twitterings in the leaves, the amplified minutiae

Of his movements. But for all of my wanting, I could not
Will him to return. So it is with the miraculous.

Knapp's Creek: A Drought Sonnet

Into her paltry coffers this year comes
From watersheds of mountain blue and green
Little but the constant insect thrum
And nothing of the music of the stream

That's made by lapping liquid tongues as they
Clean and polish cobbles into round.
Rough stones and sharpened silence stand and stay
Conspicuous in absence of that sound:

A chortling, a trickling, a laugh,
That fractured sing-song music constantly
Ringing as the mountain's cut in half
And carried downhill to the waiting sea

That must for now just wait with open mouth
For rain-starved hillsides to be carried south.

Homage to Hayden Carruth

Sitting on this cold rock in the middle
of what is a stream while it's raining
and for a little while after, the sun
warming my back, the cold of the earth
rising up through the stone
and into my clenched buttocks, I look around
to see what I can name:

Squirrel Corn, Black Birch, Basswood. Two maples,
Striped and *Sugar,* a few small *Black Cherries.*
Maidenhair Fern, as pretty a pairing of words
as is in the language.

American Beech. Stinging Nettle and it's curative,
Jewel Weed, wild damp ground relative of the *Snapdragon.*

Blackflies and three or four other flies, one
of which is probably the *Deer Fly,* and another that looks
an awful lot like a *Housefly,* but I'm five or six miles from
the nearest house, so what do I know? I know that I don't like to kill
either, old friend, but I still slap the sticky guts
out of these biting ones whenever I get the chance.

Most of what I can see, I know no name for. I know
so little, so little.

Owl Pellet

Wrapped in the soft felt of its own hair
is the skeleton of a field mouse. Hair,
bones, teeth, all of these indigestible parts
were left for me to find by a Barred Owl.
As I pick apart the pellet with fingers and knife,

I wonder at the life that was lived inside these bones,
the heart that raced inside these ribs
in its last seconds of beating, the black wet eyes
that once looked out from this thimble of a skull,
the weight of the fruits and seeds
that were chewed by these jaws and passed as pellets
through the slender intestine
that once threaded the eye of this fragile pelvis.

If I had the steady hand of a watchmaker
and a paleontologist's eye, I could reassemble
these permanent parts of an impermanent existence.
If I knew one or two secrets of life,
I could fill up this cage with breathing
and watch it run away.

The Field

1. A star stands balanced
   upon its sharpest point
   just beyond the horizon.

   On the next-to-highest branch of a red oak
   a sharp-shinned hawk is poised.

   The star rises into the sky
   and illuminates this hillside.

   With thirst and desire and one roving
   black eye the hawk waits.

   Among the purple-fringed orchids and blue-eyed grass,
   a field mouse is hides in the meadow below.

   But in a flash of talons and terrible gravity
   that Eden passes.

2. The bones of sixteen horses lie in the late-evening meadow.
   The rudders of their mandibles steer the hollow ships of skull
   on dusty courses beneath that brilliant star.

   The earth spins beneath the star,
   and the skulls sail on,

   each gathering their particular bones,
   the bleached cylindrical vertebrae,

   curved blades of ribs,

   and cavernous pelvises
   into trains and cages of clattering music.

   While the star is at its apogee the pasture fills
   with ghostly galloping

   and when it sets, the steeds
   are again scattered.

3. Thousands of monarch butterflies will spring
   from this field of milkweed, and rise above

   the bones of fallen horses,
   overcoming gravity and their own frailty.

   Nothing can be substituted, there is no solving
   for x or y in their lives.

   Like the milkweed,
   they simply scatter.

Hematite

Crow's earthen wings are the only things that keep his right
and left feet from burrowing root-like
into loose, fresh-turned soil and taking
hold, wintering over like the cut stalks of corn:
rigid, steadfast, watchful.

The fingered feathers, zipped together and anchored
in blood lift the bird from field to tree. Let scabby
Sycamore, with huge plates of leather dropping off to reveal
the living plaster, support him now. Sycamore has places to go,
but slowly; Crow is racing for shadowed fields
and roadsides, looking for the brief bloated ropes of grubs
or perhaps a fallen woodchuck to unstitch.

In lieu of his own, Sycamore's roots are good enough
for Crow, branches hold him upright
in the wind, provide a healthy vantage
for his keen, hematite eye.

The Trees Respond to Winter

Old man Sycamore has been dying since April.
As a matter of fact, he was dying all winter.
Come to think of it, he has always
been dying. Don't walk too close
or he'll corner you and bore you
with incessant talk of
this medicine or *that* treatment.
"I'm thinking of seeing a tree surgeon,"
he'll say, despite your insistence
that this is all normal. "Normal?
Normal?" he'll say, shaking his stiff limbs;
"I've tried everything for this bark
but look at it. Look at it!
Flaking and scaling all of the time
no matter what I do.
Are you telling me that *this* is normal?"

Sugar Maple is so lively and lovely
that you don't mind waiting
while she tries on her entire wardrobe.
"This green one is nice," she says,
"but I'm feeling a little more adventurous.
This is an occasion that calls for
adventure, don't you agree?
Maybe I'll wear this gold one . . .
or maybe the rust, it really flatters my figure."
Soon the floor is strewn with bright colors,
tried on and discarded.
"I know . . . red!" she exclaims,
but you know that she'll finally settle
on the gray, skin-tight number;
she wears it every year.

Norway Spruce weathers change well.
He is blessed with patience and
an immigrant's tenacity. "Things
are always basically the same," he tells you
with just the slightest hint of accent,
"Things change, but things stay the same,
if you find something that works, stick with it.
Do you know what I'm saying?
I'll say no more, I'm better off just listening.
If you listen, you learn. I've learned
lots of things just standing here.
Come back around
some time, come back and I'll tell you
some things. Not now, later."

Quaking Aspen's name doesn't suit her.
She fears nothing, bends without breaking,
moves with an animal grace. She never
quakes, but she often dances. Once
a year she puts on all of her mother's
jewelry and sways from side to side,
listening to the gentle sound of
bangles hitting one another. In this way,
she honors her mother, and
her mothers before; in this way,
they are all connected. Now,
as always, she says very little.
Go and stand near her,
but be quiet.

Mighty White Oak, open grown, is lonely
but thrives in aloneness. Uncrowded
by his brothers, he has found a deep-rooted roundness,
has become noble and complete. He wears in his hair
only the wind and the snow-
white souls of crows.
He stands upright in the winter wind,
clothing around his ankles, up to his elbows
in the sky.

Caraway

Five-and-one-half hours past the darkening of day
when the two-legged people are finally silent
the four-legged ones come out.

They move about the shadowed kitchen,
race along baseboards, skitter and skid

across bathroom linoleum and gather
what's necessary to carry them through:

some sunflower seeds, crusts of bread,
the insulation from a lamp cord, the fruits
of preparedness.

Before departing, the four-legs leave their mark
for the dreaming day-tenants to discover:
a hole in the corner of the cracker box,

a glass dish emptied of nuts, and a broken
trail of black caraway pellets, starting
at the stove, tracing along the sink, across

the backsplash, to the breadbox and back
to the stovetop, defining the well-waltzed
Formica dancing ground.

The Insect Bible

There are only two commandments
In the insect bible: *Thou shalt kill*
Or be killed and *Thou shalt not put your own needs*
Ahead of the needs of your people. Pretty simple
When you think about it, and safe.

Rules only get complicated
When they become numerous, when they play
Against and contradict each other.
Be Nice! shouts one; *Get All You Can!* begs another;
And still a third commands, *If It Feels Good, Do It!*

Perhaps such edicts are born of some error
In translation. There are those who argue that the biblical *virgin*
Is a misreading of the Aramaic or Greek
For *unwed mother* and, while having no bearing
On the holiness of Mary's firstborn, has nothing to do

With the intactness of her hymen. Too many rules
Too often interpreted lead to the paralysis
Of the well-intentioned. The wicked do as they will,
But those who are good at heart are easily stymied
By these moral checklists. If only their lives were as simple

As those of the insects:
Eating,
Mating,
Dying,
Singing their vespers until dawn.

Fathom

Every song about the ocean was written
from the surface or the shore by someone who knew nothing
of the sea, had seen only a fraction
of its moods, had only heard

that single throat-clearing song.
I am a sunken man, my lungs
filled with salt. I am suspended
in brine and anchored to the bottom.

I have seen the ocean pouring
its rich clear broth over oyster
beds and combing kelp forests into vertical order. I know
that the body of the sea is all hand.

Looking up through sixty fathoms
of water, the air inside you panics
for the surface, races toward the only light
around, leaving you emptied, suspended weightless
and alone in the whispering lullaby

of incomplete silence. For a short while,
you'll know the sodden noises: the friction of blood
in your ears, the sound of water opening and closing
around an octopus, the teeth
in the mouths of the blue sharks and dogfish raking
against each other, stropping themselves to sharpness.

Ars Poetica: New Years Day, 2000

Now I move from hedge to creek bank on my hands
and knees, sniffing out poems like a hound. I stare
at printed pages until words lose all meaning
and drip to the floor in a puddle, then I stare
at the blot until I make sense of the shape. I have renounced

the wearing of shoes, walk upon the earth with only my skin
between the soil or sidewalk and my brittle, brittle bones. I drink
from puddles and spring-pipes, eat only what I can
catch, take only what I can carry.

I have no overhead.

I stand perfectly still along the stream until the trees have forgotten
that I am not one of them, until the kudzu
grows up my pant leg and out my shirt collar and, hungering
for the light, hangs a tendril on my ear, leaps
to a low-hanging branch and threads me
into the fabric of all things.

My only task is to see.

I drag a pencil across a page and make
a few loopy marks, my celebrated and caustic shorthand. I make the squiggle
that stands for *trout*, and the one that stands for *worship* and the one
that means *wholeness*.

I make of the commonplace, a prayer.

Fellowship and Baked Goods

Unsolicited Advice

"You have to find a place to light
before you set about raising up young
ones. Make them a part of a place, bury
their afterbirth under an apple tree
in the yard, make their silent, half-
self a part of that dirt
so that they'll always be able to find
their way home. If you move

that little girl or boy around, if you fail
to fill their pockets with a handful of family
ground, that child won't ever rest, won't ever
find a place to call home, won't ever stop
thinking that they ought to be somewhere
else, someplace other, and Lord, you don't ever
want to hang a thing like that
on an innocent child."

A Beautiful Jar of Jelly

for Dwight Diller, Kirk Judd and David Morris

I grew up with people who made music, and made sense.

Rogue uncles and button-shoed aunts,
who'd come to Sunday dinner
in their proud brown coats
sewn on the treadle machine,
and fastened with mismatched buttons
rescued from other coats
that could no longer be patched.

Crow-eyed bachelor men
who lived on the hillside and always smelled
of fried potatoes and machine oil,
men who'd shave on Sunday and
always brought by a loaf of bread
or a sack of tomatoes when they
walked past the house
on their way into town,

Stern-faced Baptist ladies who'd tell us
"I know your mama" whenever we got caught
where we shouldn't have been.
Women who'd always ask after your granddaddy,
who'd say things like *"he ain't got a lick of sense"* or *"what a beautiful jar of jelly."*

Old fiddlers who had to toss their whiskers
over their shoulder so they wouldn't get
caught up in the bow,

and the older-still women
who sung murder ballads while they
swept off the back steps or
cut out biscuits with a tin can.

The finest times at our house
were summer evenings on the front porch.
I'd fall asleep on my granny's broad lap
listening to the bullfrog plunk of the banjo
and the katydid fiddle sing.

Perfect Mason

Along the brown bank of the creek
the fawn sand handed up a blue disk of glass,
a myopic lens cracked from the bottom of a quart
Ball Perfect Mason jar. I picked up the turquoise

circle and turned it over and over in my hands.
Lovely and benign, a generation
spent sleeping in the sandy bank has worn
whatever jagged edges it once wore

to a frosted smoothness. It must have been well-used
if not well-loved, the convex former inner surface
lay all one winter under half-runner beans, pressed
against bread-and-butter pickles the next:

filled and emptied and boiled and filled
and emptied again, held up repeatedly to its purpose
and only failing that final time. Lowered
into the canning bath once too often, the bottom cracked

clean of the clear blue cylinder of the sides
with a cough and the whole of the boil was tainted
by tomato sauce or blackberries, the surviving jars to be
cooled and washed and boiled again. The intact sides

of the Ball jar might have been saved to place in
the new-tilled garden over young tomatoes
the night before a final frost, when the wood
in the stove would have sizzled and popped with the coming

cold, but the perfect and useless circle was cast out
into the trash pile, a perfect stones throw from the kitchen
door. High water carried it from the backyard
to the creek, where it was hoisted again by water

to the bank where it slept buried like a mud turtle,
like the ignored and useful knowledge of the way to sew
an apron from a flour sack or how to feed a family
all winter on a summer's-worth of hard work

and vegetables packed into a cellarful
of identical blue jars.

Farmstead: Back Mountain Road

"Roof it again. Batten down. Dig in."
—*Seamus Heaney,* "Lightenings, ii"

Enter into that unwalled space, that foundation
where the hewn bones of roof and rafter
repose on the disregarded floor.

Pick your way through dead planks and dry leaves
to the corner where the table stood, where in the late-evening
glow of a coal-oil lantern forks coaxed deer

steak and potatoes into open mouths and tickled
enameled plates into a clattery kind of music. Guess
at where the bedstead stood, the island of quilt and straw

into which all but the first lives that lived
within these walls were born. Amid broken glass,
find an empty picture frame and the rotting chestnut gate

that must have been the mantle. Regard the chimney, a smoky cairn
that channeled the gray souls of dead oaks,
hand-set and mortarless, outstanding the confusion

of twisted boards that the house has become. Do not romanticize
the lessons to be learned here. Do not
ignore them.

Cakewalk at the Walker's Creek Firehall

The lure of fellowship and baked goods
has brought together the residents
of the Walker's Creek Valley to pay
twenty cents a chance to support
the Volunteer Fire Department,
and walk on a track of numbers
around a table of cakes.

My friends and I have come from everywhere
but Walker's Creek, still, the folks at the firehall
make us feel at home.

I buy a handful of reused tickets
weathered and softened
by the touch of many hands
and join the parade around the table.
The man in front of me sets pace
for this dance, hobbling in time
to the music, a cane in his left hand.

He is dressed for the occasion,
three plaids and no teeth,
and he loves us all
much more than we are prepared to accept.

He has no money, but has paid for his chance
a thousand times before
so when the music stops and the tickets are collected, I pay twice.

And finally, when the number
that is called is his,
he grins broader than the both of us,
and teeters forward to accept his prize. He won't walk
again tonight, no need to be greedy,

he'll just watch the ritual
from a folding metal chair,
a lap full of angel food,
his miracle.

Homage to Charles Wright

You are, in name and fact, a maker.

I see you with glasses
Pushed up on your forehead,
                    humming a little tune around your mouthful of questions
Making some marks on paper with a pen.

We have risen from the same ridge, you and I,
Twin Appalachian sons, brothers of the eastern plateaus,
                                total strangers.
But I know those old men you write about, my uncles
Also traded cars in Big Stone Gap, drove U.S. 23 from Johnson City to Asheville
In sunshine and snow,
                    hot biscuits in a towel on the floorboards
A battered thermos of black coffee in the front seat,
            the trunk of the '52 Buick full of Ball jars of whiskey.

They carried our poor heritage
Between their cheeks and gums, spat our brown legacy
In the direction of highway signs
                            and state troopers
On both sides of the line.

You poets come in through the servants entrance, eat only table scraps
And crusts of bread, your coarse peasant-speak lost

On the peasants, your high eloquence ringing not-quite-true
                        with the high and elegant.

Not a thing like your painters, those
Wielders of the brush and the palette knife
                                    who enter the soul through the front door,
Announcing their arrival with color and shape and form,
                                                universal in language,

Who move you more to words than any words,
Your love for them
                            and your envy
Are braided together in your displaced medium.

Whatever the reason you paint
With words, it is the hair shirt of your trade, perpetually misquoted,
Or worse: left untouched, your bindings not even cracked . . .

                                    ⌒

If you follow U.S. 219 south as far as you can go,
You'll end up on the banks of the New River
At Rich Creek, Virginia, just east of Glen Lyn.

It is a limestone country,
                            rolling pockmarked pastures and
A preponderance of Black Angus and Charolais.

The wooded hollows that carve the ridges into loaves still echo
With the cricketsong of dead fiddlers.
                                    I can hear them on clear nights,
Fifty-year-old vibrations rising through the summer air.

They say that TV and radio waves keep going for all eternity,
                    That right now in some distant galaxy
                    You could be tuning in to *Death Valley Days* or *My Mother The Car.*

I can hear the echo of the Kingsport of your youth,
The purest of that lonely music
                    rising to my ear,
From every ridge top,
Amplified and retransmitted
From three-hundred-odd miles,

                              as the crow flies,

South.

Gerard David, The Judgment of Cambyses, *1498.*
Oak Panels, 182.3 x 159.2; 182.2 x 159.4 (inside the frame).

Left

He is not used to being on this side
of the law, as his smart, scarlet judicial
robes suggest. And though he must know why
he is being punished, why
he is being escorted across the pale
pink and blue tile floor of his opulent chambers,
he seems, nevertheless, surprised. His attendant
hounds seem stupefied as well, as if

in their confusion they will continue to wait
where they are for their master,
the judged judge, to return
from the cobblestoned square
where the stout oaken table and the men
with knives to whom he has, no doubt,
sent dozens of men before,
are waiting.

Right

His crime was corruption
from the bench and his punishment was to be flayed
alive, three men with sharp knives peeling
back his living skin to reveal
a 15th-century ignorance
of human anatomy. The condemned man is strapped

to a heavy, oaken table, ropes tight
around his ankles and the table's legs, short restraining
pegs taught in his armpits. His expression is a mixture
of agony and resignation, a transparent attempt

to put a brave, clenched-toothed face
on the spectacle of which he has become the bleeding and damned
center. Around the periphery, men
are talking, a dog fervently scratches

his ear and the judge
who pronounced the sentence
over his disgraced colleague supervises the punishment, his face a diptych
of it's own: a two-sided mask of pity and disgust.

The men who are doing the flaying are simply
going about their business—one kneels near the table
the better to make his incision, another holds the knife in his teeth
to get a better grip on the limb he is peeling.

Refugees

The silver serving set and settee that brought the highest prices
could have come from any home, the tables at the auction set and spread
with the typical collectanea of a woman born in the 'teens—cast-iron cookware,
brass candlesticks, and lots and lots of cut glass. Boxes full of rolled waxed paper

and tinfoil, hundreds of spools of thread, thirty-seven unsharpened
pencils; desk and dresser drawers upturned and emptied into cardboard
and labeled for the purpose of the sale. The objects
that once orbited Mrs. Lena Brown now adrift and refugeed.

The truest life this woman led is nested in a box
tucked under one of the sale tables on the oiled plank floor,
a box of boxes of recipes, church basement favorites
that never saw the good china. The recipes

three-to-one desserts: a graham-cracker ice cream,
indoor s'mores and wacky cake to every deviled round steak.
Many were clipped from magazines and taped to index cards
with all of the good intentions of serving them one day. But

the ones that got made, the cards that are spotted with oil and egg
are the hand-written ones, uniformly copied in blue ink
in a hand that won class prizes in penmanship
when such things existed and mattered.

On a table opposite and also for sale are her plain white daily dishes,
the plates that knew what banana Jell-O ring and cheesy Spam bake were.
They are scuffed and scarred from years of use; the good plates
look box-new without a speck of gilt-edging gone.

No one in the family wanted this treasure
clipped and copied and catalogued, a grandmother's care
evident in the steady script, the neat dividers. Her recipes should be
placed in a cornerstone to a new building as a capsule to the future

from a time when good penmanship, home-cooked meals and a family table
were things of importance, and that, for a time, persevered.

February 23–Portland, Michigan

The stark bones of river trees shiver
silhouetted against a sullen sky. From the house
drift scraps of bowed music like downy, ashen ghosts.

The rain taps staccato time in the few leaves
dry enough to make a sound and then seeps
into the still-frozen ground. There is no silence,

no such thing as silence, no absence
of the noise that holds the spaces between objects
and keeps them from colliding. There is the rain,

the shattered limbs of fiddle tunes, the slow groan
of ice massaging itself back into water.

The Century Plant

for J. R. G.

I have come to think of you as the century plant, growing
just millimeters a year, keeping your compact
and prickly self low to the desert ground.

Citizens of that desolate country are so used to lack, so at home
with the everyday politics of necessity that animals move
about almost always at night and plants grow

at evenly-spaced distances from one another in order to stay
each out of the other's sphere of need. There's no lack
of scrutiny in that arid homeland, everything watched

over or baked beyond recognition by the relentless Sonoran
sun. For years, you have kept to yourself while
all those around you have blossomed

and laid themselves open to the gentle invasions of moth, bee,
bat. But you seemed to thrive, or at least survive,
in your cool and isolate distance while

all around you blazed, albeit briefly. That's what makes
your current blooming so astonishing, that after seasons
too many to count you have decided in your own time

that it is time, and have unfolded yourself to your new, true height,
crowning yourself in scarlet and declaring after so many years
of avoiding notice, of ducking praise: behold! I am here!

It doesn't really take one-hundred years for the century plant to bloom—it's just
less often, but more extravagant, than expected. Forgive me
for forgetting that. I stand before you now, amazed.

Las Palomas

In the film that is this morning
a young man walks from the dirt road
across the clear blue Mexican desert
and into the abandoned rail station. He sits
on a bench worn smooth and nearly-black by use
and places an army-surplus shoulder bag
on the seat beside him. From the bag he withdraws
a slim tan journal in which he begins to write.
Behind the station, and to the left, a plume
of dust marks the retreat of the pickup
truck that dropped him here.

The tile floor is deep with guano
and the rafters are crowded with *palomas*
"pigeons" turned beautiful
by the soul-kiss of Latino tongues.
Las Palomas have no short-term memory,
soon after the young man sits down, they resume
their isolated routine of preening and cooing.
When, after nearly an hour, he sneezes,
the birds leap into flight as if one body,
and they swirl around the building
in whirling flight, the pigeon closest to the center
barely beating a wing, those on the outer edge flapping
for all that they're worth just to keep up with the flock.

Spooked, they do not return to the station
but instead settle into the open window
of an abandoned warehouse across the tracks,

that is, all but one.
This pigeon floats toward the feet of the man on the bench
before settling lightly to the ground. This pigeon
unfolds his spindly black legs into gray linen trousers
tucks his wings into black jacket sleeves
and sits down on the bench, careful to keep the shoulder
bag between himself and the young man, who now
appears more and more like a boy.

"*Hombre*," says the pigeon man, "There hasn't been a train
through here in sixty-two years, I doubt you're going to catch one
today. You'll have better luck riding your thumb
back on the dirt road, eh?" The young man nods.
The pigeon man nods too,
then rises.

Teaching Eighth Grade Math

I want to tell them all so much,
not so much
about polynomials or how to work equations
with signed variables, but rather about the ways I know
that they can save themselves the heartache
of merely becoming themselves. I can still
remember the fear that they are trying to mask
behind indifferent faces and bleached blonde bangs.
I can still taste that terror
bitter and metallic
a flavor that diminishes but never leaves
your tongue, a flavor that grows
to be a part of the taste of your own mouth.

They try so hard to convince themselves
that they need nothing from me,
that they know all that there is to know,
that some of them succeed. The inconsolable,
unreachable ones are the ones I want to gather
into my arms and squeeze until they stop struggling,
until they break into tears and admit
that they are alone and scared—just like
in a made-for-TV movie—but
I know that my good intentions far outreach
any chance of that happening. Still,

to the pretty girl in the front row seat who smiles
coquettishly and at thirteen wears
makeup, gold rings and a delicate chain
around one pink ankle, I want to say,

slow down, it all comes fast enough. I want to tell her
to leave her face and toenails unpainted, to avoid
the high school barracudas. I want to say,
early ripe, early rot
but I don't. My own awkward history,
my fear and blunders and estrangement can teach nothing
to her, or any of them. They must unravel
their own perfect blanket
of childhood before they can truly see
the world around them, before they can make their kinked
and knotted threads into something they can hide in,
before they can realize that while they can always knit
their lives back together, it will never be
the same, or as large
or enough.

The Way It Is

See now, here's the way it is. I got this badge in 1969 and I got this hat in 1969.
Private investigator first class, agent double-oh 9.
I'm what they call a PFL.
The P is for private investigator first class.
The F is for the God-damn federal government. Federal government.
And the L is lieutenant. God-damn FBI.
God-damn secret service I am, that's right.
You gotta be military of course. God-damn army. I was there.
World-war-two veteran, I got shot too; once in Germany and once in Japan.
I got shot in the leg in Germany. Shot twice in Germany, once in the leg and once in
   the back.
God-damn mortar shell, God-damn shrapnel in Japan.

I got a steel plate in my head this big.

So they sent me home on a sixty-day furlough, sent me back home.
Now when I came back I was in the reserves, that's the way it works.
I was an MP to begin with and when I come back, they put me in charge of these
   three men, private agents, over in Virginia.

I'm not lying to you.
I say if you can't say the truth then keep your fucking mouth shut, know what I mean?
God-damn right.

So I worked for this fella for two months, two months only.
Couldn't stand the son-of-a-bitch so I quit.
Just God-damn quit.
In a month or two I get this letter from Washington, Washington DC.
Wondering what the hell I'm doing up in here.
Wondering if I wanna come back.
So I says I won't work for that son-of-a-bitch and they said OK.
And that's how I got in the FBI.
God-damn secret service, that's the kind of son-of-a-bitch I am.

Pays good money, too.
Five thousand dollars a month, you can't beat that, no sir, can't beat that with a
    stick, no sir.

Paid me thirty-eight hundred when I was a Sergeant, but now I'm a Lieutenant.
Private investigator first class. PFL. That L is lieutenant.
Yes sir, five-thousand dollars a month.
I don't spend it either, I got lots of money.
There's only three things I'll spend my money on, yes sir and that's whiskey and dope.
Marijuana.

You can have your pills and kill yourself I don't care.
That marijuana won't hurt you, no sir, won't hurt you a bit, I smoke it myself, yes sir.
But the real dope is those God-damn pills. God-damn pills, they fucking kill you,
    am I right?

Now pay attention.

I won't stand for those pills, God-damn kill you.
And drunk drivers, I won't have it.
God-damn pills and God-damn drunk drivers.

I'm gonna buy me a farm, yes sir won't have to buy wood or nothing.
I can get the money, I got money in all of these fucking banks.
I got ten-thousand dollars over in Richwood.
Richwood!

Right here's the place yes sir.
Thank you and can I ask a favor of you?
A whiskey's two dollars, could you lend me two dollars?
I'll pay you back next time I see you.
I'm not lying.
I'm not a lying man.
I say if you can't speak the truth then keep your fucking mouth shut.

The Great Slowing

Some time when the river is ice ask me
mistakes I have made.
　　　　　　　　　—William Stafford
　　　　　　　　　　"Ask Me"

Some Lessons in Poverty

Keep yourself and your family clean.
When you are invited to dinner, accept.

A glass of warm
water 20 minutes before a meal
makes a bruised orange or heel of bread
feel like more.

When you run out of cream, learn to
drink coffee black. When you run out of sugar,
learn to drink it bitter. When you run out of coffee,
learn to drink it not at all.

Buy dried beans and soak them
overnight, you'll get half-again as many beans
for the money.

Quit
smoking, even if it's your only
comfort. A pack a day is twenty-eight dollars a week and
fouteen-hundred-and-fifty-six dollars a year.

Selling blood doesn't carry
the stigma that it used to.

Blackberry

My father kept house like he kept the books
at his bank: balanced, orderly, neat. Even
his garden was prim, too prim

for tendrils or corms, and only roses were allowed
thorns. Small, five-petaled and white,
my blooming was not as expected. Armed

with his clippers, he would prune the weak
and the spindly down
to below ground if he could, hoping to weed

out every unpredictable or disappointing thing.
Season after season I raised my head
from the cultured beds of garden and house,

but small white flowers are all that I know, small white flowers
and the darkness that follows each click
of the shears.

Homunculus

Here is a boy with ash-brown
hair, hazel eyes and an almond face turned outward
in a questioning gesture. What
can I give to you, little
man? I can't walk
you back to the crinoline rustling
of garter snakes in old garden walls, can't dream
you back to tug at the topmost sheet
of the Magic Sketch pad and leave
behind only the black wax ghosts
of your mistakes: the dead catfish
left on the front porch, the small red station-wagon
ice-stormed into the utility pole, your marriage.

Little, pale, sun-licked boy
what music echoes in those seashell
ears? Even your briny singing cannot dissolve
or preserve the voiceless body
you will become.

I can no longer hear
you, but I can still see
you, reading in your upstairs bedroom that smells
of pumpernickel and plasticine clay, the upper
unpickable branches of the apple tree
brushing against the cheek of your window.

Earshot

I pushed my face through the thick film
of disbelief and snagged a mouthful of night
air. My tiny
buzzing brain could not grasp what the call
was about, but my white-knuckled fist
beat like a heart around the telephone

in my right hand. The telephone
was heavy and black like in a 1940's film.
I pried open my fist
and tried to bring the night
into focus, to make sense of the call
and my mother's tiny

voice, made more tiny
by the smooth funnel of the telephone.
The call
had come while I was watching a film
with friends on a Friday night.
I was shaking my fist

at the old man in the movie who was shaking his fist
at a judge. Could this frail, tiny
man be responsible for those atrocities that night
in Budapest, during the war? The telephone
danced in its cradle. I paused the film
and answered the call.

"*We just got a call
from your sister*," my mother's voice tight like a fist
in her throat. A film
of hot shame enveloped me. I became tiny,
a child barely able to support the weight of the telephone
against his shoulder and head. The balmy night

turned cold, like that other night
in Budapest: the young Hungarian girl tried to call
out for help as the Nazis beat down her door, no telephone
to ring a neighbor, no help in earshot. The officer's fist
smashed her tiny
porcelain face. It was only a film.

In the film that was my life that night,
I learned new atrocities: my tiny sister pinned beneath a stranger, her call
for help beaten back with a fist, my helpless hand cramped around the
      telephone.

The Portrait of My Great-Grandfather—Christmas 1986

All three living room sofas faced his picture
as if still seeking approval, as if he had the final say, as if
a starched Presbyterian sixty years dead was Jesus himself.
His sternness was the stuff of legend. A saint
in a family of holiday Christians, he feared
God and loved temperance. He despised disorder,
temptation, weakness, and me.

Even when I turned to face the tree,
I could see his angular face reflected rounder in the blue,
green and gold glass globes. From his perch
above the stocking-laden mantle he couldn't have known
that the eggnog tasted like cleaning fluid, that Uncle David was drinking
again or that Aunt Catherine hadn't eaten in days. I could
lift her over my head if only she could stand
another person's hands on her body.

Like the rest of us, my great-grandfather had no idea
that inside a silver box beneath the tree was an engagement ring
for my cousin Elizabeth or that inside my cousin Elizabeth
was his great-great-grandson, to be born the next July.

I have no memory of my great-grandfather
other than his portrait, his pious scholar's eyes staring at me down
the long nose we've all been cursed with, chiding me
for the temptations I've succumbed to, not just at the holidays,
but all year 'round: too much food, too much
drink, dark Belgian chocolates in the shapes of tiny shells.

Oneiromancy

Dreaming of silverware suggests that company is coming, a woman for each spoon, a man for each fork and a stranger for each knife. A serving spoon foretells a pregnancy.

Different bodies of water mean different things to the dreamer. A lake or pond suggests continued success, while a river or stream intuits change. A dream of the ocean bodes well for a journey.

Music in a dream is a sign of deep well-being, unless played on a harpsichord or sousaphone.

The appearance of medical personnel in a dream prognosticates fire, either a cookout or a conflagration. Look for other signs to indicate the severity of the blaze. Surgeons or Orthopedic specialists invoke the smell of grilling chops and burgers, while hygienists bode nothing but charred framing members and soft, white ash.

Some feel that a dream of clowns is a harbinger of death, while others believe that it merely prophesies the removal of a bunion or ingrown toenail.

Fine nut woods such as walnut or pecan, especially in the form of antique furniture, forecast a heated argument with a family member. Nut meats or butters suggest burgeoning racial tension.

A dream of teeth is always a bad sign. Watch your health.

The Party

It was a party in celebration of a milestone anniversary of a certain petrochemical company. Because of this fact, the invited were asked to dress only in synthetic fibers—nylon, orlon, polyester—in keeping with the company's history and the general theme.

Upon entering the rented hall, each guest was presented with a small souvenir basket of chocolates and pinned to a long, single length of cannon fuse, either at the bodice or the lapel. Soon, all of the guests were tethered to one another both by their connection to the industry and the braided fuse.

Waiters wearing white cotton caps emblazoned with a black latticed oil derrick circulated through the crowd with trays of "Molotov" cocktails: high-proof Russian vodka with a splash of kerosene for flavor, garnished with a short length of blue rag.

After the CEO had made the obligatory speech about tradition and the inherent evil of alternative fuels (in blithe ignorance of the gasohol his guests were filling up with) he turned out the lights and lit the fuse. The guests cheered as the small flame sputtered its way from torso to torso and the celebrants were immolated, one-by-one.

To someone looking in through a window, it must have looked like a birthday party at first, the room lit by candles on a cake—except for the slowly diminishing number of guests and the occasional bright yellow flare as another polyester tuxedo jacket made the violent transition from darkness to light.

After a while it was impossible to see just what was going on in the room, the air thick with smoke and the windows greasy with new-rendered fat.

Sleeping Scotland

"High above us in the night, a thousand faces sleep in flight."
—*Peter Case,* Beneath the Spell of Wheels

37,000 feet beneath this pressurized cabin
full of groggy businessmen and engine noise, a sleeping
Scotland comes into view. After the long Atlantic
crossing, the sodium vapor streetlights
that blur into a collective, hearth-like glow
are a comfort, a beacon reminding me that I am
once again in the region of people, and not merely adrift
among motionless stars. The largest
of the buildings below are bathed in golden light and stand

out as brilliant, shimmering spots, each being full, perhaps,
of sleeping people, each being indistinguishable
from any other at this altitude. Some landmarks can be made out:
municipal housing blocks, roads, the coast
of the Irish Sea, airports I will never see

from the ground. I imagine some early-rising
Scot, a baker or newspaper boy, looking up
at the pre-dawn sky and making out
the single, moving speck that stands for myself
and several hundred other souls. I like to think of him
wondering, as I am, about the lives inside that glowing
light, adrift as it is, among
the motionless stars.

Homage to Charles Simic

You are sorrowful and skeletal, Simic, old son.

Forty years in the new world;
                    New Hampshire, New York,
Have not driven dark Yugoslavia
From your blood. She will always be in you
                Like a fever,
                        like hepatitis, leaving you forever poisoned.
Broken into smaller political pieces, Yugoslavia lives yet
In your stomach
Where as a child you swallowed her, whole.

Do you really see us humans
As ants? As fragile, crushable creatures, hard
On the outside, insides brimming with instinct and goo?

Who was it who said, *'I don't believe in God,*
But I fear him,"? It could have been you for all I know,
                            and I would not be surprised.

I envy you
Your bright, exhausted eyes,
                    your shimmering rage,
Your tiny hammer hammering at the shins of God.

The Fossil Record

Given the option of drunkenness over having my eyes
filled with earth I'd still choose to live
underground: darkened, swaddled, oligochaetic.
Let the soils part as seas before my face
and cement with my castings behind me.

I have heard you singing a song
of yourself while burying me.

Dig me up, I dare you.
You will not be able to tell
which way I am headed,
which end is forward
and which end is back.

It's just as well.
As if we were actually related
by dirt, as if you really understood
the language of worms, as if any
of this even matters.

The Experimental Bowler

There are so many variables,
but she tries to account for them all:
the heft and hand-feel of the ball, the color
and roundness. Even if she finds one
that looks good, there's no guarantee
that it will fit her hand. All she can do is try

each on until she finds the one that feels
like a weighty extension of herself, a shimmering
green or purple sphere that caresses her palm with a face
like a startled pumpkin to gently take her
thumb into its mouth and hold her ring
and middle-fingers with its eyes.

Even though she winces
every time the attendant sprays disinfectant
into her rental shoes,
she always wears them. They give her
the proper combination
of traction and glide.

She savors an image of herself,
an image of herself walking away,
the thick rope of her hair swaying
like a pendulum across the small clock
of her shoulders, her footfalls ticking
into the distance without alarm.

The Haiku Moment

At first I was unaware
what it was I was, or rather wasn't
hearing. What started
as a prickling

on my neck grew into a pancake-
sized patch of amber light
on my hot pate. Then the buzzing:

a florescent light with bad ballast swarming
into a horde of Japanese beetles
descending on the first blossom. My soul rose

up with that sound, beating its wings
against the vaulted ceiling of my skull,
and my neck craned, body stretched eleven feet
to contain the enormity of this inner-noise.

Then it stopped. A circuit
breaker tripped or a movie reel broke. Silence,
devoid of birds, wind,

moving water. What came crashing
in on me were all the sounds that hadn't
been happening happening
all at once.

The Great Slowing

When my friend died
at eighty-eight, I knew
that I would miss him and his terrible silence,
but it took eleven months
to realize that I would also miss
the nursing home where he had lived.

I miss the long halls of lives,
catalogued like books in a library:
I miss the weathered gentle faces,
the quiet and the crazy and the incontinent.
I miss the smell of disinfectant and urine.
I love to be among the very old,
because I know that I will never belong
to that delicious club. I fear
that I have already gained
too much momentum and will not be able
to coast the last six-hundred yards to death's door,
but will smash into it with ferocious speed,
splintering it from its hinges and
passing through to the other side,
scattering the lobby furniture like mobile homes
in a tornadoed trailer park, penetrating
the back wall of the reception area with such force
that my atoms and those of the wall
will forge some new and unstable element.
Only then will I come to rest.

How I envy those
who approach that great slowing with
grace and foresight, consciously moving slower
and slower
as their objective comes into view, begins
to grow from a speck on the horizon
into a form they can recognize. It is too late already
for me to grasp the comforting thought,
to make my house at a point along the path
where I can look across the back fence and watch
Death mowing the lawn,
where we can exchange Christmas cards and pleasantries,
where living is a near-death experience;
so that when he finally says,
"Do you want to come over tonight,"
I can, without hesitation,
answer. "Yes."

Photographing the Dead

The way that they lie there so silent,
without even the softest whistle of breath
hands neatly folded upon satin as if
they have fallen asleep while reading a book—
they are the patient ones.

They keep to themselves, and smirk
sometimes. Behind those waxy smiles they stay
true to an oath, a multitude of secrets
are carefully kept within the fraternity
of the dead.

I linger,
and look a little too long upon them. There is too much
I want to remember, that their hands feel like eel-skin
change purses, for example.

I sometimes take their photograph.

I arrange the lighting just so,
and shoot a long exposure.

Martins Ferry

for James Wright

Who would have thought
that magic could be found in that gray barge town,
a town with one foot in the black mud
of the Ohio River and a belly full of petrochemicals
and wanting, a cemetery
of second and third chances,
a place like Martins Ferry, Ohio.

But this is a place of confluence,
a place where water meets with water and is forever
changed. A place where it's possible to stand
on the rain-soaked banks and shout
poems at that greasy river as both blessing and curse.
Our tarnished souls could meet
in that place of dirty water, wade into the river
hand-in-hand, and rise again
on the other side: reborn, forgiven
and perfectly clean.

A Meditation on Surrender

And then it comes, the hunger
for salt in your belly, the need to lick
the old wounds, the final, fruiting
desire to make peace with the dark
and mineral earth.

All that is left is forgetting.
Everything else has retreated
into a rear-view speck, blinked out
of your memory like a star winking
out at dawn. You might as well surrender

to the inviting maw
of the absolute. You mean almost nothing
to it. It will mean everything
to you. Give yourself over
to the ground, let it feel the even pressure of your body
laid out as if for burial. Let yourself feel

the cool sexual press of damp leaves into the small
of your naked back, your skin beginning to pinken
and blister as the sun reclaims it's warmth. The sound
the stream has practiced for ten-thousand years has slipped

into your ears, found a home in your head
where it can wash out every meandering
thought, leaving your skull hollow, sand-scoured
and brilliant, a vessel waiting to be filled.

Notes

Pg. 29—*Fathom* was inspired by the final scene of Jane Campion's excellent film, *The Piano*.

Pg. 34—*A Beautiful Jar of Jelly*. The images of "rogue uncles" and "button-shoed aunts" come from Kirk Judd's fine poem, *My People Was Music*, which opened my ears to the possibility of writing on paper with the voice that was in my head.

Pg. 44—*Gerard David,* The Judgment of Cambyses, *1498*. The painting from which the title of this poem comes hangs in the Flemish Primitives gallery of the Groeningen Museum in Brugge, Belgium.

Pg. 62—*Earshot*. The film mentioned is 1989's *The Music Box*, directed by Costa-Gavras, and starring Jessica Lange and Armin Mueller-Stahl.

Biographical Note

Doug Van Gundy has been an elephant keeper, a copywriter, a country radio disk jockey, a letterpress operator, an arts administrator and a TV game show winner. He has also taught composition to inmates and college freshmen, helped high school teachers integrate writing into their classrooms, led creative writing weekends for university students and has worked with poets from age 5 to 75. He earned his M.F.A. in poetry from Goddard College.

His work has been published in numerous regional literary magazines and has won prizes in both the *Eve of Saint Agnes* and *Lullwater Review* competitions. His poems have been included in the anthology *Wild Sweet Notes: Fifty Years of West Virginia Poetry*. A portion of one of his poems appeared in an television commercial for the game show *Who Wants To Be A Millionaire*.

Doug is also a well-known fiddler and banjo player, and he frequently performs and teaches old-time music as half of the duo *Born Old*. He lives in Elkins, WV.

This is his first book.